JANE AUSTEN'S
Little Book About Life

*Compiled & Introduced
by Terry Glaspey*

HARVEST HOUSE PUBLISHERS
EUGENE, OREGON

JANE AUSTEN'S LITTLE BOOK ABOUT LIFE

Text copyright © 2019 by Terry Glaspey

Published by Harvest House Publishers
Eugene, Oregon 97408
www.harvesthousepublishers.com

ISBN 978-0-7369-7675-6 (hardcover)
ISBN 978-0-7369-7676-3 (eBook)

Cover and interior design by Dugan Design Group

All images in this book were found in the British Library's collections
and are believed to be in the public domain. They can be viewed
at www.bl.uk.

Printed in China

18 19 20 21 22 23 24 25 26 27 / RRD / 10 9 8 7 6 5 4 3 2 1

The Wisdom of Jane Austen

THERE ARE PLENTY OF REASONS why so many readers love Jane Austen's novels. They tell such wonderful stories and are filled with characters that seem both a bit eccentric and, at the same time, so much like many of the people we've met in the course of our lives and loves. We chuckle and laugh at their misadventures, and we might even grimace a bit at how often they reveal something about the person who stares back at us from our mirrors.

Austen's stories are simple at heart, and she is painting on a fairly limited canvas. She isn't Tolstoy giving us the grand sweep of an era and its struggles. Instead, Jane Austen writes novels about young ladies and their search for an appropriate life partner. All the drama is created by the question of who they will or will not choose to marry. Along the way there is also plenty of subtle social commentary about the times in which Austen lived and about the problem that money—or the lack thereof—created in the search for true love. And the delightful comedy that accompanies that drama makes her books doubly memorable.

Perhaps one of the biggest reasons that true Jane Austen fans can't keep themselves from wanting to revisit these novels regularly are the pearls of wisdom they contain. Words spoken by the narrator or one of the characters that ring true for the reader—insights about love, romance, virtue, decorum, grace, and a hundred more ordinary topics that she views with extraordinary insight and gentle good humor. In this small volume I've gathered a collection of some of my favorite quotes from one of the most perceptive, witty, and generous writers who ever lived. Taken together, they provide us with some insight into Jane Austen's views about life. They are no substitute, however, for reading the novels, and I hope that perusing some of these wonderful quotes will cause you to clamber up out of your chair and pull one of her novels down off the shelf for a fresh look.

Terry Glaspey

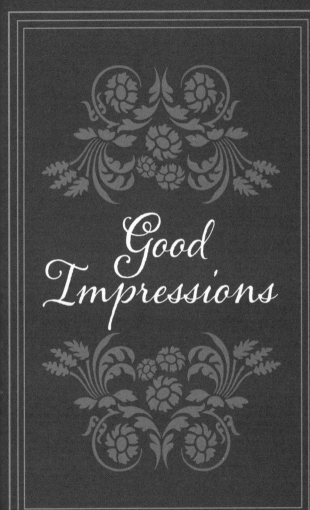

Good
Impressions

You are never sure of a good impression
being durable.

A simple style of dress is so infinitely prefer-
able to finery. But I am quite in the minority, I
believe; few people seem to value simplicity of
dress—show and finery are everything.

Mrs. Elton in *Emma*

Considering how very handsome she is, she
appears to be little occupied with it.

Mr. Knightley on Emma Woodhouse
in *Emma*

I T WOULD BE MORTIFYING to the feelings of many ladies, could they be made to understand how little the heart of man is affected by what is costly or new in their attire; how little it is biased by the texture of their muslin, and how unsusceptible of peculiar tenderness towards the spotted, the sprigged, the mull, or the jackonet.

Northanger Abbey

As for admiration, it was always
very welcome when it came, but she
did not depend on it.

Northanger Abbey

It sometimes happens
that a woman is handsomer
at twenty-nine than she
was ten years before.

Persuasion

My good opinion once lost,
is lost forever.

Mr. Darcy in
Pride and Prejudice

9

[On being "accomplished"]

A woman must have a thorough knowledge of music, singing, drawing, dancing, and the modern languages, to deserve the word; and, besides all this, she must possess a certain something in her air and manner of walking, the tone of her voice, her address and expressions, or the word will be but half deserved.

Caroline Bingley in
Pride and Prejudice

Character

There are people, who the more
you do for them, the less they will do
for themselves.

Emma Woodhouse in *Emma*

A man who has nothing to do
with his own time has no conscience in his
intrusion on that of others.

Marianne Dashwood in
Sense and Sensibility

How quick come the reasons
for approving what we like!

Persuasion

The real evils, indeed, of Emma's situation were the power of having rather too much her own way, and a disposition to think a little too well of herself.

Emma

It is particularly incumbent on those who never change their opinion to be secure of judging properly at first.

Elizabeth Bennet in
Pride and Prejudice

The more I see of the world, the more am I dissatisfied with it; and every day confirms my belief of the inconsistency of all human characters, and of the little dependence that can be placed on the appearance of either merit or sense.

Elizabeth Bennet in
Pride and Prejudice

15

Nothing is more deceitful than the appearance of humility. It is often carelessness of opinion, and sometimes an indirect boast.

Mr. Darcy in *Pride and Prejudice*

Vanity working on a weak head produces every sort of mischief.

Mr. Knightley in *Emma*

There is a stubbornness about me that never can bear to be frightened at the will of others. My courage always rises with every attempt to intimidate me.

Elizabeth Bennet in *Pride and Prejudice*

C.E. Brock
May 1895

Let your conduct be the only harangue.

Edmund Bertram in
Mansfield Park

There is no charm equal to
tenderness of heart.

Emma Woodhouse in *Emma*

There is hardly any personal defect
which an agreeable manner might
not gradually reconcile one to.

Anne Thorpe in
Northanger Abbey

I will be calm. I will be mistress of myself.

Elinor in *Sense and Sensibility*

A person may be proud without being vain. Pride relates more to our opinion of ourselves, vanity to what we would have others think of us.

Mary Bennet in *Pride and Prejudice*

Lady Middleton was more agreeable than her mother only in being more silent.

Sense and Sensibility

Silly things do cease to be silly if they are done
by sensible people in an impudent way.

Emma Woodhouse in *Emma*

We are sent into this world to be as extensively
useful as possible, and where some degree of
strength of mind is given, it is not a feeble
body which will excuse us—or incline us to
excuse ourselves.

Diana Parker in *Sanditon*

Friendship

It is not time or
opportunity that is
to determine intimacy;
it is disposition alone.
Seven years would be
insufficient to make some
people acquainted
with each other, and seven
days are more than
enough for others.

Marianne Dashwood in
Sense and Sensibility

There is nothing I would not do for
those who are really my friends. I have no
notion of loving people by halves,
it is not my nature.

Isabella Thorpe in
Northanger Abbey

Friendship is certainly the finest balm for
the pangs of disappointed love.

Northanger Abbey

It is my unhappy fate seldom to treat
people so well as they deserve.

Letters of Jane Austen

I dearly love a laugh… I hope I never
ridicule what is wise or good.

Elizabeth Bennet in
Pride and Prejudice

Where there is a disposition to dislike, a
motive will never be wanting.

Lady Susan in *Lady Susan*

Love & Romance

It is a truth universally acknowledged,
that a single man in possession of
a good fortune, must be in
want of a wife.

Pride and Prejudice

♡

Anything is to be preferred or
endured rather than marrying
without affection.

Letters of Jane Austen

♡

Matrimony and dancing…in both,
man has the advantage of choice,
women only the power of refusal.

Henry Tilney in
Northanger Abbey

People that marry can never part, but
must go on and keep house together.
People that dance only stand opposite each
other in a long room for half an hour.

Catherine Morland in
Northanger Abbey

If there is anything disagreeable going on,
men are always sure to get out of it.

Mary Musgrove in *Persuasion*

Warmth and tenderness of heart,
with an affectionate, open manner,
will beat all the clearness of head in
the world, for attraction.

Emma Woodhouse in *Emma*

LOVE, THEY SAY, is like a rose;
I'm sure 'tis like the wind that blows,
For not a human creature knows
  How it comes or where it goes.
It is the cause of many woes:
  It swells the eyes and reds the nose,
And very often changes those
  Who once were friends to bitter foes.

From a poem by Jane Austen

Men of sense, whatever you may choose to say, do not want silly wives.

Mr. Knightley in *Emma*

A woman in love with one man cannot flirt with another.

Catherine Morland in
Northanger Abbey

She began to now comprehend that he was exactly the man who, in disposition and talents, would most suit her.

Elizabeth Bennet of Mr. Darcy in
Pride and Prejudice

If I could but know his heart, everything would become easy.

Marianne Dashwood in
Sense and Sensibility

I suppose there may be a hundred different ways of being in love.

Emma Woodhouse in *Emma*

C.E.Brock

Sense will always have attractions for me.

Elinor Dashwood in
Sense and Sensibility

❧

To be sure, you knew no actual good
of me—but nobody thinks of that when
they fall in love.

Elizabeth Bennet in
Pride and Prejudice

❧

He expressed himself on the occasion as
sensibly and as warmly as a man violently in
love can be supposed to do.

Pride and Prejudice

To you I shall say, as I have often said before, do not be in a hurry, the right man will come at last.

Letters of Jane Austen

A fortnight's acquaintance is certainly very little. One cannot know what a man really is by the end of a fortnight. But if *we* do not venture somebody else will.

Mr. Bennet in *Pride and Prejudice*

Husbands and wives generally understand when opposition will be vain.

Persuasion

I cannot think well of a man who sports with any woman's feelings; and there may often be a great deal more suffered than a stander-by can judge of.

Fanny Price in *Mansfield Park*

To marry for money I think the wickedest thing in existence.

Catherine Morland in *Northanger Abbey*

That is their duty, each to endeavor to give the other no cause for wishing that he or she had bestowed themselves elsewhere.

Henry Tilney in *Northanger Abbey*

C E Brock
1895

Your countenance perfectly
informs me that you were in
company last night
with the person whom you
think the most agreeable in
the world, the person
who interests you at this
present time more than all
the rest of the
world put together.

Mrs. Smith in *Persuasion*

♡

It is better to know as little as possible
of the defects of the person with
whom you are to pass your life.

Charlotte Lucas in
Pride and Prejudice

42

I pay very little regard to what any young person says on the subject of marriage. If they profess a disinclination for it, I only set it down that they have not yet seen the right person.

Mrs. Grant in *Mansfield Park*

♥

I lay it down as a general rule that if a woman doubts as to whether she should accept a man or not, she certainly ought to refuse him.

Emma Woodhouse in *Emma*

♥

I assure you, I have no notion of treating men with such respect. That is the way to spoil them.

Isabella Thorpe in *Northanger Abbey*

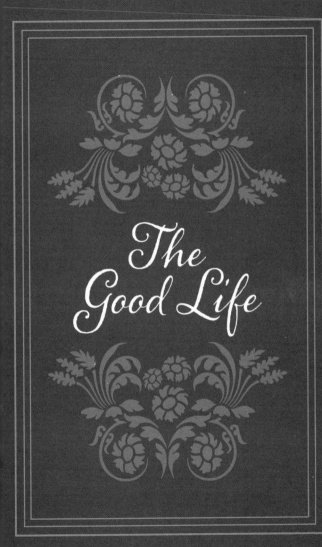

The
Good Life

One man's ways may be as good as
another's, but we all like our own the best.

Admiral Croft in *Persuasion*

Surprises are foolish things.
The pleasure is not enhanced, and
the inconvenience is often
considerable.

Mr. Knightley in *Emma*

The pleasantness of an employment
does not always evince its propriety.

Elinor Dashwood in
Sense and Sensibility

C E Brock

We all have our best guides within us,
if only we would listen.

Fanny Price in *Mansfield Park*

Nothing ever fatigues me but doing
what I do not like.

Miss Crawford in *Mansfield Park*

There will be little rubs and
disappointments everywhere,
and we are all apt to expect too much;
but then, if one scheme of happiness
fails, human nature turns to another;
if the first calculation is wrong, we
make a second better: we find comfort
somewhere.

Mrs. Grant in *Mansfield Park*

Nobody minds having what is
too good for them.

Mansfield Park

Laugh as much as you choose,
but you will not laugh me
out of my opinions.

Jane Bennet in *Pride and Prejudice*

My idea of good company is the
company of clever, well-informed
people who have a great deal
of conversation.

Anne Elliot in *Persuasion*

Her own thoughts and reflections were
habitually her best companions.

Mansfield Park

How wonderful, how very wonderful
the operations of time, and the changes
of the human mind!

Fanny Price in *Mansfield Park*

Do not give way to useless alarm;
though it is right to be prepared
for the worst, there is no occasion
to look on it as certain.

Mr. Gardiner in
Pride and Prejudice

They are much to be pitied who have not been given a taste for nature in early life.

Edmund Bertram in
Mansfield Park

Know your own happiness. You want nothing but patience—or give it a more fascinating name, call it hope.

Mrs. Dashwood in
Sense and Sensibility

To sit in the shade on a fine day, and look upon verdure, is the most perfect refreshment.

Fanny Price in
Mansfield Park

*E*lizabeth continued her
walk alone, crossing field after
field at a quick pace, jumping
over stiles and springing
over puddles with impatient
activity, and finding herself
at last within view of the house,
with weary ankles, dirty stockings,
and a face glowing with the
warmth of exercise.

Pride and Prejudice

There is nothing like staying at
home for real comfort.

Mrs. Elton in *Emma*

I wish, as well as anybody else,
to be perfectly happy; but
like everybody else,
it must be in my own way.

Elinor Dashwood in
Sense and Sensibility

It was a delightful visit; perfect,
in being much too short.

Emma

For what do we live, but to
make sport for our neighbors, and
laugh at them in turn?

Mr. Bennet in *Pride and Prejudice*

I must learn to brook being happier
than I deserve.

Captain Wentworth in *Persuasion*

It is very difficult for the prosperous
to be humble.

Emma

$\mathcal{S}$eldom, very seldom,
does complete
truth belong to any
human disclosure;
seldom can it happen that
something is not a
little disguised, or
a little mistaken.

Emma

I do not want people to be very
agreeable, as it saves me the trouble of
liking them a great deal.

Letters of Jane Austen

Life seems but a quick succession
of busy nothings.

Fanny Price in Mansfield Park

If things are going untowardly
one month, they are sure to
mend the next.

Mr. Weston in Emma

An interval of meditation,
serious and grateful, was the best
corrective of everything dangerous.

Persuasion

Every moment has its pleasures
and its hope.

Mansfield Park

[Mrs. Weston's] situation was
altogether the subject of hours of
gratitude and of moments
only of regret.

Emma

Wisdom is better than wit, and
in the long run will certainly
have the laugh on her side.

Letters of Jane Austen

Provided that nothing like useful knowledge could be gained from them, provided they were all story and no reflection, she had never any objection to books at all.

Of Catherine Morland in
Northanger Abbey

The person, be it gentleman or lady, who has not pleasure in a good novel, must be intolerably stupid.

Henry Tilney in
Northanger Abbey

With a book he was regardless of time.

Of Mr. Bennet in
Pride and Prejudice

And to all this she must yet add
something more substantial, in the
improvement of her mind
by extensive reading.

Mr. Darcy in
Pride and Prejudice

Oh! I am delighted with the book!
I should like to spend my whole
life in reading it.

Isabella Thorpe in
Northanger Abbey

A fondness for reading, properly
directed, must be an education in itself.

Mansfield Park

It is very worthwhile to be tormented
for two or three years of one's life, for the sake
of being able to read all the rest of it.

Henry Tilney in *Northanger Abbey*

For my own part, if a book is well
written, I always find it too short.

"Catherine, or the Bower" (juvenilia)

I am not at all in a humor for writing;
I must write on till I am.

Letters of Jane Austen

I DECLARE AFTER ALL there is no enjoyment like reading! How much sooner one tires of anything than of a book! When I have a house of my own, I shall be miserable if I have not an excellent library.

Miss Bingley in
Pride and Prejudice

An artist cannot do anything slovenly.

Letters of Jane Austen

Indulge your imagination in every
possible flight.

Letters of Jane Austen

I think I may boast myself to be,
with all possible vanity, the most
unlearned and uninformed female who
ever dared to be an authoress.

Letters of Jane Austen

Faith

I hope I am properly grateful to the Almighty
for having been so well supported.

Letters of Jane Austen

Pardon, O God, whatever Thou has seen
amiss in us, and give us a stronger desire of
resisting every evil inclination and weakening
every habit of sin.

The Prayers of Jane Austen

Thou art everywhere present, from Thee
no secret can be hid. May the knowledge of
this, teach us to fix our thoughts on Thee,
with reverence and devotion that we
pray not in vain.

The Prayers of Jane Austen

Give us a thankful sense of the
blessings in which we live, of the
many comforts of our lot;
that we may not deserve to lose
them by discontent or indifference.

The Prayers of Jane Austen

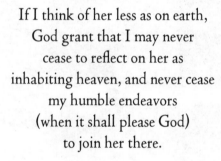

If I think of her less as on earth,
God grant that I may never
cease to reflect on her as
inhabiting heaven, and never cease
my humble endeavors
(when it shall please God)
to join her there.

Letters of Jane Austen

INCLINE US, O GOD, to think humbly of ourselves, to be severe only in the examination of our own conduct, to consider our fellow-creatures with kindness, and to judge of all they say and do with that charity which we would desire from them ourselves.

The Prayers of Jane Austen

The Providence of God
has sustained me.

Letters of Jane Austen

May the Almighty
sustain you all.

Letters of Jane Austen

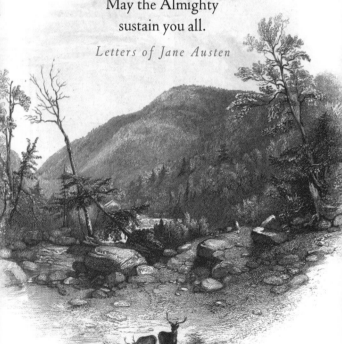

You
Might Also
Enjoy...

THE PRAYERS
of JANE AUSTEN

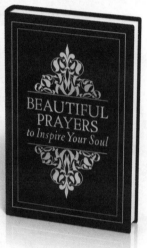

BEAUTIFUL
PRAYERS
to Inspire Your Soul